POSITIVE STEPS

Caring for Others

Susan Martineau

with illustrations by Hel James

W

FRANKLIN WATTS
LONDON • SYDNEY

 An Appleseed Editions book

First published in 2011 by Franklin Watts
338 Euston Road, London NW1 3BH

Franklin Watts Australia
Hachette Children's Books
Level 17/207 Kent St, Sydney, NSW 2000

© 2011 Appleseed Editions

Created by Appleseed Editions Ltd,
Well House, Friars Hill, Guestling,
East Sussex TN35 4ET

Designed and illustrated by Hel James
Edited by Mary-Jane Wilkins
Picture research by Su Alexander

ISBN 978 1 4451 0361-7

Dewey Classification: 177.7

A CIP catalogue for this book is available from the British Library.

Picture credits
Contents page Jupiterimages/Thinkstock; 4 Monkey Business Images/Shutterstock;
5l Stefanolunardi/Shutterstock, r Monkey Business Images/Shutterstock;
6 Michaeljong/Shutterstock; 7 DenisNata/Shutterstock; 8 Martin Poole/Thinkstock;
11t Photodisc/Thinkstock, c & b Jupiterimages/Thinkstock; 12 & 13 Thinkstock;
14 Jupiterimages/Thinkstock; 15 Comstock/Thinkstock; 16 Jupiterimages/
Thinkstock; 17 Thinkstock; 18t BananaStock/Thinkstock, b Thinkstock; 19 Brasiliao/
Shutterstock; 20 Pixland/Thinkstock; 21 Thomas Northcut/Thinkstock;
22 Thinkstock; 23t Comstock Images/Thinkstock, c Jupiterimages/Thinkstock,
b Shutterstock; 24l Jupiterimages/Thinkstock, r Thinkstock; 25 Jupiterimages/
Thinkstock; 26t ©UNICEF/NYHQ2006-1591/Noorani, b Shutterstock;
27 BananaStock/Thinkstock; 28-29 Lakov Kalinin/Shutterstock;
32 Greenland/Shutterstock
Front cover Palmer Kane LLC/Shutterstock

Printed in Singapore

Franklin Watts is a division of Hachette Children's Books,
an Hachette UK company.
www.hachette.co.uk

Contents

My brother is kind to me.

What does caring mean?

Caring for others means thinking about other people and not always putting ourselves first. When we care for others we think about what they might need or how they are feeling.

We need to care for each other at home, at school and when we are out and about. Have a look through the book to see all the different ways we can do this.

LET'S TALK ABOUT...

Look at these words. They are all about caring for others. Can you think of any more words like this?

considerate

kind

sympathetic

Share your games and toys.

Let everyone join in.

Help round the house.

5

Being a good friend

We all like having fun and being happy with our friends. Good friends also care about us and will help us when we are not so happy. Katie is writing to her best friend Ally, who used to live next door.

Dear Ally
I wish you were still here.
My mum and dad are splitting up and I am scared about what will happen next. I feel like crying all the time. I'm so worried that nothing will ever be the same again.
Write soon.
Love from
Katie xx

When families split up it is hard for everyone. It is normal to feel upset and worried. Katie needs to be able to talk to a good friend who will try to **understand** how she is feeling.

Can you think of times when you have been unhappy and your friends have shown how much they care about you?

I fell over and hurt my leg.

We fetched help.

My pet died.

I was really sad when my dog died.

Don't worry, your mum will be better soon.

What can you do?

- Notice if your friends are **upset**.

- Be sympathetic and listen to them.

- Try to imagine how they feel.

- Try to cheer them up.

Helping round the house

A family is like a team. We need to think about how our actions affect everyone else in that team. Being **thoughtful** and helpful shows we care about the others in our family.

The more you help, the less nagging there will be.

OK Mum.

Can you please tidy your room Ben.

There are all sorts of jobs that need to be done around the house. We should not expect other people to do the ones we could easily do ourselves, such as putting clothes away and being tidy.

put my shoes away

hang up my towel

make my bed

The help chart

You could make a chart of jobs you could do each day. Ask your mum or dad what would be most helpful. Perhaps you could do a chart for other people in your family too, so everyone takes their turn.

LET'S TALK ABOUT...

Can you think of ways you can help around the house? The list of jobs might be very long, but don't be put off. The more you help, the quicker those boring jobs will get done. There will then be more time for everyone to do fun things.

Ben's Help Chart
Monday Put my clothes away
Tuesday Feed the cat
Wednesday Tidy my room
Thursday Clear the table
Friday
Saturday
Sunday

I'll play with the baby

If you have a younger brother or sister you can help to care for them. This is especially helpful when your mum or dad is trying to get something else done, such as cooking a meal or phoning someone.

It can be fun thinking of games to play with younger children. You have to remember that they are only small, so you always need to be gentle with them.

Can you play a game with Bella while I get the food ready?

I'll do that clapping game she loves.

LET'S TALK ABOUT...

Your younger brother or sister will think it's great when you play with them. Can you think of other ways you can help with little ones?

read a story

help at bath time

play a game

The story game

Think of your favourite story and make up some actions to go with it. Ask your teacher if you can visit the children in the younger years of your school and perform the story for them.

Working together

Classrooms are busy places. There need to be some rules to make sure they don't get too noisy or messy! Following these rules shows we care about the others in the class.

I was using that ruler.

Imagine a football game without any rules. A class is like a football team. Everyone has a part to play and everyone needs to keep to the rules.

We've got lots to do today, so listen carefully.

LET'S TALK ABOUT...

Imagine if there were no school rules. That might sound like fun, but you would never get anything done. Rules are a way of helping everyone get along. Can you think of some good rules?

TEN TOP TEAM RULES

1 Listen politely and quietly to the teacher.

2 Ask to borrow things — don't grab.

3 Take turns and don't be bossy.

4 Don't shout out.

5

6

Ten top team rules

Make a large poster of ten rules for your class. You can add some for your teacher too!

13

Thinking of others

When friends come to play we show we care about them by asking them what they would like to do. We **share** games and toys and make them feel welcome in our home.

Sometimes friends will say they don't mind what they do, but it is still important to ask them.

What do you and your friends like doing best? Can you think of some great games to play when they come round? Do you know what your friends' favourite snacks are so you can have them ready?

What can you do?

● Be polite and considerate to visitors. Say hello and goodbye.

● Share your toys and games.

● Ask visitors if they would like something to eat or drink.

● Think of some good games or activities for your guests.

This is Arjun's favourite juice.

It's so lovely to see you.

I'll get help

Accidents sometimes happen. They can happen at home, at school or when we are out and about. We all need to know what to do if there is an accident.

What can you do?

These are the responsible **actions** to take when someone has an accident:

- Find the teacher or grown-up in charge.

- Someone should stay with the hurt person.

- Tell the hurt person that help is on the way.

If someone breaks a window or a piece of school equipment you need to find the teacher or grown-up in charge and let them know.

Emergency action!

Think of a pretend **emergency** scene. Act out what to do after someone has fallen over and hurt themselves. Remember to do it carefully so no one really gets hurt. Be **responsible**!

I use a wheelchair

Sarah uses a wheelchair because she has a **disability** that means her legs don't work properly. She gets fed up when people stare or point at her. Sometimes people fuss over her, but there is no need because she can look after herself really well.

When buildings have lots of stairs Sarah needs to find a lift or ramp for her wheelchair. Ramps are special sloping paths.

Don't worry Sarah. There must be a ramp somewhere.

Yes, or a lift?

What can you do?
At Sarah's school there are ramps and extra-wide doors so it is easy to get around. Have a look round your school and see if someone in a wheelchair could move round it easily.

Painting challenge
Some people have disabilities that mean they can't use their hands to do things. Can you write your name holding a pen or paintbrush in your mouth or between your toes?

Letting everyone join in

James has a learning disability. He has a special person to help him in the classroom but he finds it hard to join in with the other children.

I'll get there first!

Come on. Bet you can't beat me!

I wish I could play too.

Sometimes the other children laugh at James and call him names. He feels as if they really do not care about him. He would like to join in their games.

If you have a learning disability it means you find it hard to learn or do some things. Perhaps you have a learning disability yourself or you know someone who has one.

What can you do?

● Try to understand how it might feel to have a learning disability.

● Never make fun of or bully anyone with a learning disability.

● Think of games that **include** everyone.

Caring for older people

Older people can sometimes find it hard to get out and about. Sam's granny lives alone and loves it when he visits her.

Dear Sam

Thank you so much for coming to see me. I did enjoy our chat and visiting the park with you.

Thank you, too, for posting those letters for me on your way home.

Come again soon. It was lovely to see you.

Lots of love
from Granny xx

Can you imagine how it might feel to be elderly? Can you think of ways you would like others to care for you if you were not able to go out very easily?

carry some shopping

Hello Grandad. How are you?

ring up for a chat

help in the garden

Stories from the past

Older people can tell us lots of interesting things about the past and how things used to be. You could ask a grandparent or elderly relative to tell you some stories. You could even write down their stories and draw some pictures.

23

Looking after our world

Our beautiful planet Earth is the only home we have. We need to work together to care for it. There are many ways we can do this, both at home and at school.

Taking action is the only way we can look after our world. If everyone has a go then it really will make a difference.

Recycle paper, cardboard and plastic.

Adopt an endangered animal.

LET'S TALK ABOUT...

You may be taking action for the planet already. Talk about it to your friends and family so they know how they can make a difference too.

Don't leave taps dripping. It wastes water.

Action for others

A charity is a group of people who raise money to help others. Charities help people who are poor, ill or disabled, or who have suffered a disaster like an earthquake or a flood.

We're raising money for children who have no clean water.

There are many different charities, or good causes, to help or **support**. Some of them work in our own country and some help people in other parts of the world. Some charities also work to save the **environment** or endangered animals.

I'm learning how to talk in signs.

Sign language is a way of talking to people who are deaf or can't hear well.

Perhaps your school or class already supports a charity. Can you think of charities you have heard of or perhaps seen on the television? Talk about the charities you would like to help.

Making a difference

Ask your teacher if you can hold a special charity day to raise money for your favourite charity. Think of all the different ways you could do this.

Get everyone to pay to dress up for a day!

Sell unwanted games and toys.

Tell all your friends and family.

What can you do?

Look at these words. Write them down. Now think of something you, or someone you know, has done to put them into action. For example, perhaps you have been sympathetic to a friend who was feeling sad.

sympathetic

thoughtful

polite

kind

responsible

helpful

understanding

I'm sorry you're feeling sad.

Think of ways to help other people.

Listen to your friends when they need to talk.

Words to know

action
Something that you do.

considerate
Thinking about what other people would like and about their feelings and needs.

disability
Having a disability means you cannot use a part of your body properly because of illness or an injury. A learning disability makes it difficult to learn things in the same way as everyone else.

emergency
An emergency is an unexpected and serious event, such as an accident, when help is needed very fast.

endangered
In danger. Endangered animals are in danger of dying out.

environment
The world around us.

include
To let someone join in and be part of what you are doing.

recycle
To make rubbish into things we can use again.

responsible
Taking charge of something yourself and doing something on your own.

share
To let other people use your things.

support
To help someone.

sympathetic
Being sorry for someone and showing that you care when they are upset.

thoughtful
Thinking about what other people would like.
Putting their feelings first.

understand
To be able to imagine how someone feels and what it means to them.

upset
Very sad and unhappy.

Index

Friends care about each other.